A New True Book

WORK ANIMALS

By Kathryn Wentzel Lumley

This "true book" was prepared under the direction of Illa Podendorf, formerly with the Laboratory School, University of Chicago

CHILDRENS PRESS, CHICAGO

Belgian plow horses

Allan Roberts—2, 7, 9, 13 (3 photos), 18, 19, 37, 41 (right)
Lynn M. Stone—4, 6, 17, 22, 25, 43
Hillstrom Stock Photos—© Ray Hillstrom, 32
© Milton and Joan Mann, Cover
Julie O'Neil—10 (top), 34 (left), 39, 41 (left)
Ruth Welty—29
James M. Mejuto—10 (2 photos, bottom), 15
James P. Rowan—23
Finland National Tourist Office—27 (2 photos)
Chandler Forman—30
Art Thoma—34 (right)
Jerry Hennen—45
COVER—Ox cart, Mekong River, Thailand

Library of Congress Cataloging in Publication Data

Lumley, Kathryn Wentzel.
  Work animals.

  (A New true book)
  Includes index.
  Summary: Briefly describes the work performed by a variety of animals around the world, including dogs, cats, llamas, zebras, and yaks.
  1. Working animals—Juvenile literature. [1. Working animals] I. Title. II. Series.
SF172.L85   1983   636.08'86   83-7511
ISBN 0-516-01711-X   AACR2

Copyright© 1983 by Regensteiner Publishing Enterprises, Inc.
All rights reserved. Published simultaneously in Canada.
Printed in the United States of America.
1 2 3 4 5 6 7 8 9 10 R 92 91 90 89 88 87 86 85 84 83

TABLE OF CONTENTS

The First Working Animals... 5

Horses... 8

Donkeys, Burros, and Mules... 12

Cattle... 15

Camels... 21

Reindeer... 26

Elephants... 28

Cats... 31

Dogs... 33

Birds... 43

Animals Help Us... 45

Words You Should Know... 46

Index... 47

Wolf

THE FIRST WORKING ANIMALS

Did you know that a long time ago all animals were wild? There were no pets or friendly animals. Then people found that some animals could be trained to work for them.

One of the first animals to work for people was the wolf. Cavemen knew that

Bison facing wolves. Wolves hunt in packs.

wolves hunted and ate the same animals that people did—wild pigs, reindeer, and bison.

When cavemen heard the howling wolves, they followed them. It saved the hunters a lot of work and time.

Eventually some hunters took young wolf cubs home and tamed them. Then men and wolves hunted together!

The dogs we love today are relatives of those wolves who worked for cavemen and played with their children.

Newfoundland dogs were used as lifesavers pulling people from ocean waters.

HORSES

Before there were any automobiles, tractors, or trucks, horses did the work those machines do now.

A long time ago wild horses were caught and used to pull war chariots. Later people tamed horses and rode on their backs.

Horses and ponies

A hundred years ago horses pulled plows, stagecoaches, streetcars, and delivery trucks. They pulled lumber wagons, fire engines, and carriages.

Ponies, called pit ponies, carried coal out of the mines.

When the United States was young, horses carried the mail out West to places where there was no railroad. This was called the Pony Express.

Today horses are used for pleasure, riding, racing, rodeos, movies, and horse shows. Cowboys still ride horses on the range.

Some horses are trained to dance. The dancing white horses of Vienna are called Lipizzaners.

DONKEYS, BURROS, AND MULES

The horse has relatives that have worked for people for thousands of years. The donkey and burro are used as beasts of burden in Spain, Italy, and Mexico.

A mule's mother is a horse and its father is a donkey. Mules are very strong. They are about the size of a horse.

The mule (above), the donkey (left), and the burro (below right) are used to carry heavy things in many countries of the world.

In the Andes Mountains of South America mules haul gold and minerals from mines. They also carry packs or riders. Mules work on plantations and in lumber camps. They do not get excited easily and often move only when they want to move. That is why some people are called "stubborn as a mule."

Oxen

CATTLE

Oxen are very strong animals. Early Egyptians used oxen the way later farmers used horses.

The ox has a relative, the water buffalo, that also

Water buffalo

works hard. Female water buffalo are milked. The bulls do the hard work. In Iraq you can tell how rich a man is by the number of water buffalo he owns.

The yak lives on the highest mountains in the world, the Himalayas in

Yak

Asia. It is one of the biggest animals in the ox family.

The yak has long shaggy hair. It is strong and can live in very, very cold weather. It grunts like a pig, but looks like an ox, so it is called a "grunting ox."

Brown swiss cattle are raised for their milk and meat. They can be used for work, too.

Cows give milk that helps keep us healthy. It is used in treats like ice cream and pudding, too.

Cows helped the farmer do his work, and also provided food for his family.

A zebu looks large and fierce, but it is gentle.

A cowboy rides a Brahma bull in a rodeo.

Zebus are sometimes called Brahma cattle, or humpbacked oxen. They have humps on their shoulders. Cowboys try to ride zebus in rodeos.

Brahma bull from India

In Asia zebus are used as pack animals and to pull plows.

In India the white zebu is sacred. The Hindu religion says that no one should harm it. It goes wherever it wants to go and does whatever it wants to do.

CAMELS

The camel is called "the ship of the desert" because it can travel across the desert as easily as a ship travels on the sea. It has long, powerful legs. The pads on its feet keep it from sinking in the sand. Strong eyelids keep sand out of its eyes. The nostrils in its nose are tiny to keep sand out of its lungs.

Dromedary camel

  The camel's hump has muscle and fat that can be used for food. The pockets in its stomach store water. A camel can go for as long as five days without water and with very little food.

  Camels can travel as far

Bactrian camels

as fifty miles a day. They carry heavy loads.

Camels with two humps are called Bactrian. They live in Central Asia. The dromedary, or Arabian camel, has only one hump. It lives in North Africa, India, and Arabia.

Working camel on a desert in China

Camels work for people, but most people do not like them. Camels have bad tempers and they are not smart.

The llamas of South America belong to the camel family. They are used as beasts of burden.

Llamas

 Their wool is used to make blankets and clothing.
 The llama has a better temper than the camel. Sometimes, however, when it is tired, it will spit at its master!

REINDEER

Reindeer seem to have built-in snowshoes. They can walk on top of the snow. They do not mind cold weather. Reindeer have hair on the end of their noses to keep them from freezing.

In northern North America, Europe, and Asia, reindeer pull sleds and carry people and

Reindeer are work animals in many countries.

things on their backs. People could not live in these cold places without reindeer to work for them.

In North America reindeer are also called caribou.

ELEPHANTS

Elephants, the largest land animals on earth, live in Asia and Africa. Elephants are huge! They can be as tall as thirteen feet and can weigh as much as fourteen thousand pounds.

Elephants have very tough, thick skin. Sometimes they are called pachyderms, which means thick skin.

Elephant moves teak logs in a forest in Thailand.

Asian elephants have been taught to carry heavy teak logs on their tusks. They take them down the mountains. Then they put the logs in rivers to float down to lumber mills.

When the logs get to the mills, other elephants take them out of the water. Elephants can even stack boards after the logs are sawed.

Asian elephants often work in the circus. They can do many tricks and are fun to watch.

Circus elephants usually are Asian elephants.

CATS

If you have ever had a cat, you know what a good friend it can be. Cats work for people by doing what they do best—catching rats and mice.

In Egypt as long ago as 3000 B.C. cats kept rats away from grain. They were so helpful that they were thought of as gods.

In England cats worked in post offices to keep rats

and mice out. They were fed as pay for their work.

Tame cats are still working hard to keep rats and mice out of homes, barns, and other buildings.

It is nice to have a pet that works so hard.

DOGS

Man's best friend, the dog, has worked since the days of early wild dogs and wolves. Men and dogs hunted together and helped protect each other.

Today, dogs hunt with their masters for sport. Most dogs are pets or companions.

There have been more than a thousand different breeds of dogs. Today about two hundred breeds are popular.

German shepherds and English collies are used to

The collie (above) and the German shepherd (left) are good work animals.

help herd animals. They keep them from wandering away when they are in the fields and hills. They round up the flocks and take them home.

Some dogs are detectives. Bloodhounds help the police find people who are lost. They can track down criminals by following their scent.

Many cities now have dogs as part of their police force. German shepherds are the most popular because they are smart, big, and easy to train

In the snow-covered Arctic dog teams pull sleds across the ice and snow with blizzards howling around them. The dogs carry people, mail, and supplies.

Siberian husky mother with her pup

When the dogs are harnessed to a sled, the dog in front is the leader. The dogs have no reins on their harnesses. The driver talks to them and they obey. If one dog slows down and doesn't pull hard, the other dogs growl at him. When they are out of harness, the other dogs snarl and nip at the lazy one. The next day he works as hard as the rest.

A seeing-eye dog is trained to be the eyes for a blind person. A guide dog helps its blind owner lead a very full life. It protects, guides, and loves its blind friend.

Golden retrievers can be trained to be guide dogs.

Dogs also work with people who cannot hear. They let deaf persons know when the phone or door bell rings.

Dogs help people who are in wheelchairs or must stay in bed. They bring them clothes, slippers, mail, newspapers, and other things. Often they are the hands and feet for these people. What good friends dogs are!

In Switzerland, Saint Bernard dogs help save lost travelers. They dig them out of snowdrifts and bark for help.

The St. Bernard puppy (left) and the dalmatian (above) can be trained to help people.

Many people keep dogs to guard their homes. Dogs are good friends and good helpers, too.

Dogs have been used during wars to carry messages through enemy lines. They worked as guards at prison camps and supply stations. They could sniff out buried mines that the enemy hid to blow up people.

Dogs are intelligent. They are willing workers. Dogs work in television and movies. Benji and Lassie are two famous movie dogs. How many others can you name?

Whether they are little or big, dogs help people in many ways.

This red-tailed hawk, named Lisa, has been trained to hunt.

BIRDS

Not all hunters have four legs and fur. Strong, swift birds can be trained to hunt small animals.

Hawks live in America, Asia, Africa, and Europe.

When they are caught as babies, they can be trained. When a hawk obeys, its master gives it food. It takes a lot of patience to tame big birds.

Eagles and owls have been taught to hunt. A Chinese golden eagle can even catch wolves and foxes.

These birds are called birds of prey because they hunt other animals for food.

ANIMALS HELP US

Since the beginning of time, animals have worked for people. Whether they hunt, carry people and goods, pull heavy loads, entertain us, or are our friends and pets, animals make life easier and more fun.

WORDS YOU SHOULD KNOW

beast of burden (BEEST UV BER•din) — an animal that is used to carry goods
breed (BREED) — a particular type of animal
chariot (CHAIR•ee•ut) — a two-wheeled cart pulled by horses
nostril (NOSS•trill) — either of the two outer openings of the nose
pachyderm (PACK•ih•derm) — any of the thick-skinned animals
prey (PRAY) — an animal hunted or caught by another animal for food
sacred (SAY•crid) — something that is thought of or treated with special respect; holy
scent (SENT) — odor; smell
surly (SER•lee) — bad-tempered; rude

INDEX

Africa, 23, 43
Andes Mountains, 14
Arabia, 23
Arabian camels, 32
Arctic, 36
Asia, 17, 20, 23, 26, 28, 43
Asian elephants, 29, 30
Bactrian camels, 23
Benji, 42
birds, 43, 44
birds of prey, 44
bison, 6
blind person, dogs for, 38
bloodhounds, 35
Brahma cattle, 19
breed of dogs, 34
burros, 12
camels, 21-24
caribou, 27
cats, 31, 32
cattle, 15-20
cavemen, 5-7
Central Asia, 32
Chinese golden eagles, 44
circus elephants, 30
collies, 34
cowboys, 11, 19
cows, 18
dancing horses, 11
deaf persons, dogs for, 39
dogs, 7, 33-42
donkeys, 12
dromedaries, 23
eagles, 44
Egypt, 31
Egyptians, 15
elephants, 28-30
England, 31
English collies, 34
Europe, 26, 43
foxes, 44
German shepherds, 34, 36
"grunting ox," 17
guard dogs, 41
guide dogs, 38
hawks, 43, 44
Himalaya Mountains, 16
Hindu religion, 20
horses, 8-11, 12, 15
humpbacked oxen, 19
India, 20, 23
Iraq, 16
Italy, 12
Lassie, 42
Lipizzaners, 11
llamas, 24, 25
Mexico, 12
mice, 31, 32
movie dogs, 42
mules, 12, 14
North Africa, 23
North America, 26, 27
owls, 44
oxen, 15, 17, 19

pachyderms, 28
pigs, wild, 6
pit ponies, 9
police dogs, 35, 36
ponies, 9
Pony Express, 11
rats, 31, 32
reindeer, 6, 26, 27
Saint Bernard dogs, 40
seeing-eye dogs, 38
sled dogs, 36-38
South America, 14, 24

Spain, 12
Switzerland, 40
television dogs, 42
United States of America, 11, 43
Vienna, 11
wars, dogs in, 41, 42
water buffalo, 15
white zebus, 20
wild animals, 5, 6, 8, 33
wolves, 5-7, 33, 44
yaks, 16, 17
zebus, 18-20

About the Author

Kay Lumley is a nationally known reading specialist, and author of numerous books and articles on reading and its teaching. She is a graduate of Lock Haven State College (Pa.) and the Pennsylvania State University. Last year she received the Distinguished Educator Award from the L.H.S.C. Alumni Association. Her experience includes teaching and supervision at all levels from elementary through university classes, and director of The Reading Center for the Washington, D.C. Public Schools. Mrs. Lumley is a member of the Reading Is Fundamental (RIF) board of directors. She is a trustee of the Williamsport Area Community College, Williamsport, Pa., and is an active participant in leading professional and civic associations. She lives near her son, Joe, in Rauchtown, Pa. with many assorted animal friends.